Be the Boss of your Sleep

Self-Care for Kids

Timothy Culbert, M.D., and Rebecca Kajander, C.P.N.P., M.P.H.

"The most useful and wise book series for children that I have ever seen."
—**Lonnie Zeltzer, M.D.**

Director of Pediatric Pain Program, UCLA Mattel Children's Hospital

"Practical, enjoyable ways to enhance [children's] self-care abilities. Has positive implications for an entire lifetime."
—**Karen Olness, M.D.**

Professor of Pediatrics and Director Emeritus, Developmental/Behavioral Pediatrics Department at Rainbow Babies and Children's Hospital, Cleveland, Ohio

"Clear, practical . . . excellent series on self-care for kids. I recommend it highly."
—**Andrew Weil, M.D.**

Director, Program in Integrative Medicine, University of Arizona, and author of *8 Weeks to Optimum Health*

free spirit
PUBLiSHiNG®

Helping kids
help themselves™
since 1983

V08

CL

Library of Congress Cataloging-in-Publication Data
Culbert, Timothy.
  Be the boss of your sleep : self-care for kids / Timothy Culbert and Rebecca Kajander.
      p. cm.—(Be the boss of your body series)
  ISBN-13: 978-1-57542-255-8
  ISBN-10: 1-57542-255-7
  1. Sleep—Juvenile literature. 2. Sleep disorders in children—Prevention—Juvenile literature. I. Kajander, Rebecca. II. Title.
  RA786.C85 2007
  613.794083—dc22

                                                                    2006103284

The concepts, ideas, procedures, and suggestions contained in this book are not intended as substitutes for professional healthcare.

The people depicted on the cover and throughout this book are models and used for illustrative purposes only.

Edited by Eric Braun
Illustrated by Tuko Fujisaki
Cover and interior design by Calico

10 9 8 7 6 5 4 3 2 1
Made in China

Free Spirit Publishing Inc.
217 Fifth Avenue North, Suite 200
Minneapolis, MN 55401-1299
(612) 338-2068
help4kids@freespirit.com
www.freespirit.com

Free Spirit Publishing is a member of the Green Press Initiative, and we're committed to printing our books on recycled paper containing a minimum of 30% post-consumer waste (PCW). For every ton of books printed on 30% PCW recycled paper, we save 5.1 trees, 2,100 gallons of water, 114 gallons of oil, 18 pounds of air pollution, 1,230 kilowatt hours of energy, and .9 cubic yards of landfill space. At Free Spirit it's our goal to nurture not only young people, but nature too!

Dedication

To Heidi, Samuel, and Hannah, with all my love, and to William and Joanne Culbert, with special thanks for their love and support. —T.C.

For Laura, my yoga teacher, for helping me use mind/body/spirit skills in my daily life. —R.K.

Acknowledgments

Our continuing respect and gratitude to the pioneers of pediatric mind-body-spirit skills: Drs. Karen Olness, Daniel Kohen, Judson Reaney, Candace Erickson, Lonnie Zeltzer, and Leora Kuttner. Thank you to Dr. William Manahan, Cathy McMahon, and Michael McMahon, for reading and commenting on drafts of the book. We'd also like to extend our gratitude to Judy Galbraith for supporting this important project, as well as to Eric Braun and the entire fun-loving team at Free Spirit Publishing for their ability to turn our ideas into reality. Finally, thanks to all the wonderful and talented children and families with whom we have been privileged to collaborate and from whom we have learned so much.

Contents

Important Note (Don't Skip This!) 1

★ Your Body Is Amazing! 2

You Can Be the Boss of Your Body! 4

How Will This Book Help Me? 4

Be the Boss of Your Sleep 5

★ What It Means to Be the Boss of Your Body 6

What Is Your Body? 6

What Is Your Mind? 7

What Is Your Spirit? 7

How Balance Can Help 8

The Power of the Positive 10

Who's the Boss? 10

★ Whew, I'm Tired 12

Why Do You Need All This Sleep Anyway? 13

Sleep Problems 14

How Do Sleep Problems Affect You? 16

What Can You Do? 16

★ Checkup for Your Body, Mind, and Spirit 18

What Are Your Sleep Problems Like? 20

Brain/Body Scan 20

Rate Your Body, Mind, and Spirit 22

How Would You *Like* to Feel? 24

Take Control of Sleep **26**

Get Comfy! 27

B³ Skill 1: Belly Breathing 28

B³ Skill 2: Imagine That! 30

B³ Skill 3: You're the Coach 34

B³ Skill 4: Self-Suggestion 36

B³ Skill 5: Aromatherapy 38

B³ Skill 6: Acupressure 42

B³ Skill 7: Massage 46

Keep Practicing 47

Feel Good Every Day **48**

Move More, Feel Better: Exercise 48

Eat Well and Feel Super: Your Diet 49

Give Yourself a Break: Life Management 49

Take Care of Your Inner Self: Spiritual Stuff 50

Connect with People: Social Supports 51

Keep Track of Your Progress 52

Stick with It 52

A Note to Grown-Ups **54**

About Self-Care Skills 54

Your Role as a Coach 54

Glossary 56

About the Authors 56

Important Note (Don't Skip This!)

In this book you'll learn ways to take charge of your health. But even though you're the one taking charge, it's still a good idea to get parents or other family adults involved, too. Show them this book, including the "Note to Grown-Ups" on page 54. Let them know how you're feeling and how it's going. You also can ask them to help you practice the skills you're learning, make changes to your lifestyle, and celebrate your successes!

Super Important Part: This book doesn't replace the need to use healthcare professionals, like doctors and nurses. It's true that you'll be happier and healthier if you are the boss of your body and can take care of most of your sleep problems on your own, but sometimes you need help. Be sure to tell your mom, your dad, or another adult when you have problems sleeping—they can help you decide if you should see a doctor. You can use the list on the next page to help you decide.

See a doctor if:

- your sleep problems are getting worse

- your sleep problems last more than a few weeks

- snoring keeps you or others awake at night

- others notice that you stop breathing briefly while you sleep

- you are sweating a lot while you sleep

- you start wetting the bed

- you fall asleep often during the day, or get really grumpy or have trouble concentrating

- you are missing a lot of school

- you start feeling very sad, worried, or nervous about your sleep problems

- you feel like nothing is ever going to make it better

- your sleep problems make you less safe (like if you're sleepwalking or thrashing about)

If you're not sure whether you should see a healthcare professional, go ahead and do it. It's better to be safe about your health than to wonder if things will get better. When you do see professionals, tell them you want to use the **self-care** approaches in this book. They will be happy to know you want to help yourself!

Self-care means just what it sounds like: things you can do your**self** to take **care** of yourself.

Your Body Is Amazing!

Everybody feels lousy from time to time. They get sick or have aches and pains, or they have trouble sleeping. Sometimes they get stressed out or just plain-old down in the dumps. Kids who feel bad sometimes believe only grown-ups—like doctors, nurses, or parents—can help them feel better. Some people may think only pills, shots, or surgery can help.

Those things *are* important at times. But wouldn't it be nice if you could make your*self* feel better—without a trip to the doctor or a bunch of medicine? What if you could do it just by taking care of yourself and believing that you will get better?

Your **body, mind**, and **spirit**—working together—have amazing abilities to heal you. You already know your body can take care of itself by healing wounds, killing germs, and fighting infections. It's like you have a hospital inside you that knows how to keep you healthy. But did you know you can also control how your body feels—even when you're having trouble sleeping?

Your body, mind, and spirit are the three main parts of yourself. Turn to pages 6–7 to learn more.

HOSPITAL
EMERGENCY

3

You Can Be the Boss of Your Body!

It's true. Being the boss of your body means knowing that your body, mind, and spirit are connected and work together. It also means knowing how to use those connections to make yourself feel better and stay healthy. It's a way for you to be actively involved in your own health and wellness.

How Will This Book Help Me?

Practicing the skills and activities in this book can help you:

✓ sleep better

✓ make fewer visits to the doctor's office, emergency room, or hospital

✓ avoid taking sleeping pills

✓ feel better for school, sports, hobbies, and other activities

✓ have more fun with friends and family

Be the Boss of Your Sleep

Part of being the boss of your body is being the boss of your sleep. This book is filled with ideas, activities, and skills you can use to fall asleep faster, stay asleep, and solve problems like being scared or uncomfortable, so you can feel well rested and energized every day. You can use what you learn in this book for the rest of your life.

When you see the abbreviation B^3 in this book, don't be confused—it's not a vitamin, an algebra problem, or a bingo square! B^3 is our shortcut way of saying "*Be the Boss of Your Body.*"

You can do most of the activities and skills with nothing more than a positive attitude and practicing every day. But there are tools, like stress balls and pinwheels, that can help you do the activities better and keep track of your progress. If you have the "Be the Boss of Your Body Kit," you already have those tools. If you don't have the kit, don't worry! You can do most of the skills and activities without any tools, and you may be able to find some tools around your home.

We wrote this book to help you be the boss of your body, and we'd like to hear how it goes for you. You can email us at help4kids@freespirit.com or send us a letter at:

Free Spirit Publishing, 217 Fifth Avenue North, Suite 200
Minneapolis, MN 55401-1299

Let's get started!

5

What It Means to Be the Boss of Your Body

Being the boss of your body does **not** mean being **bossy** to other people!

Most kids think they are healthy if they brush their teeth, don't eat too much candy, and are not sick. And it's true, those are signs of good health, but being healthy is a lot more than just having a physical body that is fit and well. It's also having a healthy, positive mind and spirit. Your body, mind, and spirit are connected and work together. Being the boss of your body means taking charge of all three to help yourself deal with common problems and feel your best.

What Is Your Body?

You know what your body is. It's the physical part of yourself—all of your bones, muscles, organs, and everything else about you that takes up space in the world. You know your own body better than anyone else. You know your strengths and weaknesses, and you know how you feel when you are healthy or sick.

When you eat well, exercise, get enough rest, and manage stress, your body runs well and fights off illnesses. You stay healthy. The reverse also is true—if you don't take care of your body, it has a harder time staying healthy.

6

What Is Your Mind?

Your mind is the part of you that thinks, understands, remembers, imagines, and feels emotions. When you picture an image in your head or try to figure out a problem, you're using your mind. You're also using your mind when you think thoughts, or "talk" to yourself in your head. That's called **self-talk,** and having positive self-talk is a great way to keep your mind healthy, fit, and happy.

I am going to sleep well tonight!

What Is Your Spirit?

"Spirit" can mean a lot of different things. In this book we are not talking about ghosts, and we're not talking about school spirit. We're talking about something inside you that gives you feelings of hope, comfort, and peace. Your spirit connects you to things outside yourself and gives life meaning. For many people, a healthy spirit has to do with a belief in God or a higher power. A healthy spirit can also come from a feeling of connection with music, art, or nature. Spiritual health is a feeling you have inside of being content or peaceful.

How Balance Can Help

When your body, mind, and spirit are all healthy and positive, they help each other *stay* healthy and positive. When this happens, we say the three are "balanced." That means they are fit and strong—each in their own way but also together—to make a whole, healthy, fabulous you!

What does it feel like to be balanced?

YOUR MIND

* You have positive thoughts and emotions.

* You feel confident, loved, grateful, proud, and safe.

* You feel organized and able to focus attention.

YOUR BODY

YOUR SPIRIT

* You have warm fingers and toes.

* Your breathing and heartbeat are regular.

* The palms of your hands are dry.

* Your muscles are relaxed.

* You notice and appreciate beauty.

* You feel connected to and loved by others.

* You have a sense of peacefulness.

* You enjoy nature.

* You may feel some identification with God or a higher power.

* You may engage in regular practice of meditation or prayer.

The Power of the Positive

If sleep troubles are making you feel lousy, the best way to get back to feeling your best is to do things that will help your body, mind, *and* spirit. People who

+ eat well and get enough exercise
+ think positively and believe they can help themselves
+ feel hopeful, peaceful, and supported by loved ones

sleep better and feel more refreshed and energized by sleep. They get sick less often, and they recover quicker from sickness and injury.

Who's the Boss?

You are the boss of your body. You can control your heart rate, breathing, hand temperature, and muscle tension—and other things that help you relax and feel better—just by thinking about them.

You are the boss of your mind. You can create positive and calming thoughts and control negative emotions and worried thoughts. All thoughts and feelings affect how your body feels.

You are the boss of your spirit. You can take a walk in a favorite place; pray or meditate; or sing, play, or listen to music, all of which can help your body feel good.

You are the boss of your life. People who do self-care skills and activities, and who are balanced in all three areas, usually live longer and healthier lives.

To successfully be the boss of all these things, it's important that **you** make the choice to do it. Learn self-care skills and activities for yourself, not for your mom or dad or a doctor or nurse, because your own motivation is what makes you successful. That doesn't mean you don't need coaching, love, support, and advice from family, friends, healthcare providers, or teachers. It just means you have to do this for you.

Whew, I'm Tired

When you're tired, your body gives you a pretty clear message: Your eyes and limbs feel heavy, it's hard to concentrate or make decisions, and nothing sounds better than to slip into a warm, comfortable bed and close your eyes. The message is, "Time to hit the sack!"

People spend a lot of their lives sleeping, especially young people. During the first two years of life, babies sleep more than half of their lives—about 13 of their 24 months are spent asleep! Over the next three years, kids sleep 50 percent of the time. Between ages five and 18, kids still sleep about 40 percent of the time!

Just about every living thing on Earth needs sleep: Humans, goldfish, cockroaches— even plants and bacteria alternate between times of rest and activity!

Why Do You Need All This Sleep Anyway?

In some ways, sleep is a mystery. Scientists haven't figured out exactly why humans need to sleep or exactly what happens to us during sleep. Many scientists believe sleep is a time to:

Fix wear and tear. The body, mind, and spirit restore themselves after being busy all day. You heal and grow.

Help learning and memory. Your brain organizes information you learned during the day and stores it in the memory parts of your brain, where it can make connections with other parts of your brain.

Save energy. Taking a break from seeing, hearing, smelling, tasting, and touching keeps you fresh.

Some or all of these ideas may be true. What we know for sure is that kids need about nine to 11 hours of uninterrupted sleep a night to restore and refresh their body, mind, and spirit.

"Totally Tired!"

Sleep Problems

Most of the time, it's easy to fall asleep when you're tired. But sometimes you might have trouble falling asleep, staying asleep, or both. Or you might sleep enough hours at night but still feel drowsy during the day. About 25 percent of kids experience some kind of sleep problem during childhood.

Problems **falling asleep** might be caused by

- being afraid
- not being tired enough (physically or mentally)
- too much stimulation late in the evening (like from TV, videos, computer time, music, exercise, or soft drinks with caffeine)
- being uncomfortable
- being too warm or too cold
- the room not being dark enough

Problems staying asleep might be caused by

- physical problems, like pain, itching, or a stuffy nose

- being worried, angry, or feeling other strong emotions

- being too warm or too cold

- too much light

- illness

- noise

- a disorder called obstructive sleep apnea (AP-nee-uh) syndrome (OSAS), which causes breathing problems at night

Some sleep problems should be checked out by a doctor. If you have serious problems paying attention or feeling very tired during the day—or if you begin wetting the bed, snoring loudly, sweating a lot while you sleep, or having very restless sleep—you should get professional help. You might have OSAS or narcolepsy, which a doctor can help treat.

Being sleepy during the day might be caused by

- not getting enough sleep

- getting sleep of poor quality (maybe because of OSAS)

- illness or pain that drains the body's energy

- the brain controlling its wake and sleep balance wrong (this is called narcolepsy)

How Do Sleep Problems Affect You?

If you're having trouble with sleep, you might start feeling bad in lots of ways—especially if the troubles go on for a long time.

Body: You might have low energy or a slow reaction time, not eat much, be less coordinated, or get sick easily.

Mind: You might get in a lousy mood; have lots of negative thoughts; or be bored, worried, or unable to focus.

Spirit: You might feel disconnected, unable to appreciate art or beauty, less interested in life or the world, or hopeless; you might wonder if you are being punished by God or the world.

What Can You Do?

Using the connections between your body, mind, and spirit, you can do lots of things to make sleep come easier—or harder.

Things That Help You Sleep Better

- Going to bed and getting up at the same time every day
- Getting lots of exercise (but not right before bed)
- Doing things to help you relax, like listening to quiet music
- Eating healthy (see page 49)
- Feeling safe, peaceful, and happy
- Sleeping in a very dark room and getting exposed to natural light as soon as possible in the morning
- Rhythmic motion, like rocking
- Soft white noise, like a fan running or a sea-sounds CD

Things That Make Sleep Harder

- Not going to bed and getting up at the same time every day
- Worrying about sleep
- Expecting sleep to be bad or get worse
- Feeling fearful, sad, or angry
- Stress
- Eating too much unhealthy food and not enough healthy food (see page 49)
- Not getting enough exercise
- Pain

You will learn B³ skills on pages 26–47 to help you be more relaxed and able to sleep at night.

Checkup for Your Body, Mind, and Spirit

If you've been having sleep problems, you know what it's like to be tired. You might feel grumpy, cloudy-headed, distracted, bored, or just lousy. But sleep affects your body, mind, and spirit in a lot of ways, including some you may not have thought of. To really understand how sleep problems are keeping you unbalanced, give yourself a **whole-self checkup.** Then you can begin to change things for the better using B³ skills.

First, think about how sleep problems affect your days. Are you too tired to do things you normally do? Are there things you usually enjoy but that aren't very fun when you're tired? Look at the list on the next page and put a checkmark next to all the things poor sleep makes harder or impossible, or just less fun for you. At the bottom of the list, add any other things that sleep problems interfere with. Make more lines if you need to.

Lousy sleep interferes with these things in my life:

☐ playing or working on the computer
☐ doing fun things with my family
☐ concentrating on homework
☐ going to my place of worship
☐ being alert during the day
☐ doing activities or sports
☐ enjoying art or music
☐ playing with friends
☐ being out in nature
☐ enjoying hobbies
☐ going to school
☐ watching TV
☐ eating
☐ other_____
☐ other_____
☐ other_____

Imagine how great it will be when you can do these things without sleep problems getting in the way!

What Are Your Sleep Problems Like?

Describe what happens on a bad night—a night when you have sleep problems. How is it different from a good night?

_____

_____

_____

_____

What other feelings or problems is poor sleep causing? Do you feel exhausted during the day? Do you feel dizzy or sick to your stomach? Do you have diarrhea? Are you less or more hungry than usual? Do you feel sad, scared, bored, or angry? This is the place to write down **anything** you think has changed because of your sleep problems.

_____

_____

_____

_____

Brain/Body Scan

Ask a parent, brother or sister, or friend to help you with this activity, which can help you be more aware of how you're feeling. Lie down or sit in a comfortable chair and have your helper read the following paragraph to you. The person should read in a calm, steady voice, pausing between sentences to give you time to think about them. Become more and more aware of your body as you go. It should take three to five minutes to do.

Think about how your body feels in lots of different ways. Starting with your head and moving slowly down your body to your toes, notice your muscles: Are they tight or loose? Sore or comfortable? Heavy or light feeling? Think about your skin: Is it dry or moist? Warm or cool? Smooth or rough? Notice how your clothing feels against your skin: Tight, loose, smooth, rough, scratchy? Notice the chair you're sitting in or the floor or bed you're lying on, and become aware of how it feels against your body: Where do you feel the most pressure? Is it soft or hard? Next, notice your heart beating. Notice your breathing. Notice the thoughts that pass through your mind, but try not to judge or react to them—just let them pass through. Notice light and shadows in the room. Notice smells and sounds, or silence.

What did you learn while you were doing this exercise? Was it hard to stay focused? If you want, write what it felt like in a journal or notebook, or draw a picture about it. As you repeat this exercise in the future, you may notice that you become more aware of how your body feels.

If you can't find a helper right now, you can do this alone. Read the activity to yourself a few times, then close your eyes and spend three to five minutes going through the activity as you remember it.

Rate Your Body, Mind, and Spirit

It's time to really think about how your body, mind, and spirit are doing. You can do that by looking at the three measuring sticks on the next page: the **Body-O-Meter,** the **Mind-O-Meter,** and the **Spirit-O-Meter.** For each one, read the description on both ends of the meter and give yourself a rating from 0 to 10. If you want to, write your score in your journal.

Body~O~Meter

You feel energetic, relaxed, pain free, comfortable, or just right.

10
9
8
7
6
5
4
3
2
1
0

You feel tense, tired, painful, uncomfortable, or just not right.

Mind~O~Meter

You have mostly positive, helpful thoughts and feelings, like happiness, pride, and confidence.

10
9
8
7
6
5
4
3
2
1
0

You have mostly negative or unhelpful thoughts and feelings, like anger, sadness, and boredom.

Spirit~O~Meter

You feel connected to others, nature, or a higher power such as God.

10
9
8
7
6
5
4
3
2
1
0

You feel lonely, out of touch, like life doesn't have meaning.

23

How Would You *Like* to Feel?

Now that you know how you feel, think about how you would *like* to feel. Of course you would like to feel better—but what does that mean, exactly? It's time to set some specific goals for yourself.

To start, imagine a good night. Think about this in very specific ways, with lots of details. How would this night be different from your bad nights? How would you feel? What exactly would happen from the moment you get into bed until the morning?

Write down your ideas:

Now imagine a good day—a day that follows a night of good rest. How would this day be different from today? What would you do that you can't do now? How do you want to feel? Think about some of the things you do every day, like eating, going to school, and playing with friends. How will these things be different on your good day? Will they be easier or more fun? Why?

Write down your ideas:

_____
_____
_____

Now write down three specific, important things you will do when your sleep is under better control:

1. _____
_____

2. _____
_____

3. _____
_____

Take Control of Sleep

It's time to learn the B³ skills and start practicing them! It's best to practice all of the skills several times so you can figure out which ones you like using and which work best to help you sleep better.

If you can, try the skills the first few times when you are *not* suffering from sleep problems—it's easier to get the hang of them that way. But if you have sleep problems now, that's okay. Jump right in!

Practice the skills two or three times a day and at bedtime until you are comfortable with them. The B³ skills are just like other things you have learned and gotten good at, like writing your name or riding a bike. The more you practice, the better you get at it and the easier it is. And once you've got the B³ skills down, they'll be there to help you forever.

Get Comfy!

You'll have better luck with these skills if you make yourself as comfortable as possible before you begin—especially if you're doing them right before (or in) bed:

- Wear clothes that are loose and comfortable.

- If you like music, put on music that is quiet and familiar. Otherwise, make sure it's quiet, so there are no distractions.

- Turn the lights low or off.

- Make sure you have a chair, pillows, blankets—whatever you like to keep yourself comfortable.

- Give yourself some privacy by choosing a place where nobody will bug you.

What About Things I'm Already Doing?

If you are already taking medicine, doing physical therapy, seeing a doctor or psychologist, or getting other helpful treatments, keep doing those things. Some kids who use B^3 skills can reduce the amount of medicine or other treatments they need, but it's important to be careful about making changes. Talk with your doctor, therapist, or whoever is helping you to make sure you are getting all the treatment you need.

Skill 1: Belly Breathing

You already know you can control your breathing—you can hold your breath, and you can breathe fast or slow. Belly Breathing is a way of controlling your breathing to make yourself feel better. It's a really easy way to calm yourself, relax your body, mind, and spirit, and—if you do it at bedtime—to slide more easily into sleep.

When to Use It: Use Belly Breathing regularly to keep your body, mind, and spirit healthy and balanced and to help yourself relax whenever you're having trouble getting to sleep. You can also use it when you haven't slept well the night before to feel less tired and edgy.

Why It Can Help: Belly Breathing relaxes your muscles, calms your nerves, helps clear your mind, and helps release chemicals (called *endorphins*) in your body that make you feel good.

What You Need: You need a comfortable place to sit or lie down.

How to Do It:

1. Imagine you have a balloon in your belly.

2. Put your hand on top of your belly.

3. Breathe in slowly through your nose, counting to three and feeling the balloon fill with air.

4. Breathe out slowly through your mouth, counting to five and feeling the balloon get flat. Imagine that the pain goes out of your body as you breathe out.

5. Notice how your muscles relax as you breathe out. Imagine a picture of your muscles relaxing.

Everyone breathes at a different rate, but most kids breathe about 20,000 times every 24 hours.

One way to make **Belly Breathing** more fun—and to help you see the results—is to use items such as a pinwheel, bubbles and bubble wand, or even a harmonica! While you are exhaling slowly you can do one of the following:

* Keep the pinwheel spinning for three to four seconds.

* Blow out through the straw part of the pinwheel (just take the top off) to help slow down your breathing.

* Blow long, slow streams of bubbles from the soapy wand.

* Sustain a note while blowing on the harmonica for three to four seconds.

B³

Skill 2: Imagine That!

It might seem hard to believe, but changing what you're thinking about can completely change the way you feel.

When to Use It: Use Imagine That! regularly to keep your body, mind, and spirit healthy and balanced, and to help yourself relax whenever you're having trouble getting to sleep.

Why It Can Help: Your mind is like a supercomputer that controls your body—and you can program your brain's "software." Creating pleasant, positive, healthy images in your mind can help you feel relaxed and can stop you from thinking about your sleep problems. It can also help you drift off to sleep more easily.

What You Need: You need a comfortable, quiet place.

How to Do It: Sit or lie down in your comfortable place. Then, as a warm-up, do the first exercise below, "Let your brain be a TV." That will help you get the hang of using the power of your imagination. Then try each of the exercises that follow. As you do these, keep in mind that they work better the more involved your brain is, so give your brain plenty of details. Imagine lots of colors, shapes, and objects. Hear pleasant sounds, smell smells that please you, and notice what you can touch or what touches you. Make it all comforting and relaxing.

Let your brain be a TV. Imagine this: your brain is a TV and YOU are in charge of the remote control! Close your eyes and imagine that you turn on the TV and see your favorite food. What does it look like? Notice lots of details. Now change the channel and see your best friend, or a parent or brother or sister who makes you happy. Next, see your favorite character from a book, TV show, or movie. See? You can change the channel. That means you can change your thinking to help yourself relax, feel better, and get to sleep easier.

Imagine fun. Imagine you are somewhere that is fun, safe, and pleasant for you. Picture yourself doing something you really enjoy, like playing a sport, reading a book, or playing with a dog or cat. Remember to imagine lots of details. As you do this, notice how your body feels. Is it relaxing? Many positive images can help you feel more relaxed, so you may want to experiment with different ones until you find the pictures that help you the most.

B³

Ride down to sleep.

Imagine you are riding in your bed down an escalator or elevator with clear walls. It's a peaceful, comforting ride down, lower and lower, into levels of an imaginary place. Outside the walls you see beautiful flowers, waterfalls, trees, or whatever you like—whatever makes you feel relaxed and comfortable. Notice that as you go lower things become more and more peaceful and quiet, the air grows softer and cooler, the lights grow dimmer. You feel safe and calm. As you glide down you feel drowsy, relaxed, and content. You enjoy the comfort and peace of this place, and you know you can drift off to sleep whenever it feels right to just let that happen.

Use the jettison technique. "Jettison" means getting rid of something by throwing it away from you. Hold a stress ball, or something soft you can safely squeeze in one hand (like rolled-up socks, a beanbag, or a small pillow). Then think of all the stress and tension and sleep-stopping thoughts that have built up inside you. Start squeezing the ball or object in your hand and imagine all that sleep-stopping stuff is traveling from your brain, down your arm, into your hand, and being squeezed right out of your hand into the ball! Then gently toss the ball onto a chair or the floor. Notice how quickly and gently your sleep can find you now, and how easily you can slide into pleasant dreams.

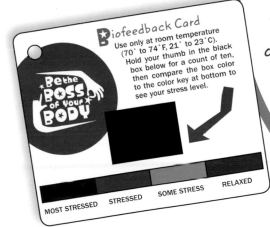

Biofeedback Card
Use only at room temperature (70˚ to 74˚F, 21˚ to 23˚C). Hold your thumb in the black box below for a count of ten, then compare the box color to the color key at bottom to see your stress level.

Be the BOSS of your BODY

MOST STRESSED   STRESSED   SOME STRESS   RELAXED

If you have a biofeedback card (you can get one at most drug stores), use it to see how your body changes as you do these imagination exercises. Biofeedback cards measure the temperature of your finger or thumb, which tells you how much stress you're feeling. Colder fingers mean more stress (and more stress means it's harder to sleep). Before you start, check your finger temperature. Then practice one of the **Imagine That!** exercises on pages 30–33 for three to five minutes and check your finger temperature again. Did it go up, go down, or stay the same? For most kids, the more you do imagination exercises, the less stress you'll feel—and the warmer your fingers and hands will get!

Self-talk is how we talk to ourselves while we are doing things. You can use positive (helpful) self-talk to help you manage difficult situations. Think of this as being a good coach to yourself. You can improve your thinking, increase your ability to relax, and be healthier by practicing positive self-talk.

When to Use It: Use You're the Coach regularly to keep your body, mind, and spirit healthy and balanced. Use it right at bedtime if you're having trouble getting to sleep. You can also use You're the Coach whenever you are feeling down about not being able to sleep, or when you're tired during the day and need extra energy.

Why It Can Help: Scientific studies have shown that your thoughts affect how your body feels. Pleasant thoughts mean feeling good!

What You Need: You need a positive attitude and a commitment to practice.

How to Do It: If you have a negative thought, replace it with a helpful one. It sounds simple, and it is—but you have to believe in the new thought, and you have to keep practicing. Hear your self-talk voice, and listen to it.

Here's a chart to help you think of some ideas. If you have a negative thought like one of those on the left side of the chart, you can replace it with the thought across from it on the right. Don't stop there, though. Think about all the negative thoughts you have and how you can turn each one into a helpful thought.

IF YOU THINK:	TRY THINKING:
I can't sleep.	I will help myself to sleep better.
Lousy sleep will ruin my day.	I will have a good day no matter what!
I know I won't sleep well tonight.	I will use my breathing and imagery to relax and sleep easily and comfortably.
I'm so tired.	I am healthy and can take care of myself even if I am tired.
There's nothing I can do to sleep better.	I will listen to my body and take care of it in healthy ways. There ARE things I can do.

FUN FACT

About 300 thoughts a minute go through a person's brain.

Skill 4: Self-Suggestion

Self-Suggestion is just what it sounds like: you make suggestions to yourself. In other words, you tell yourself how you want to feel. Using Self-Suggestion, you can create a feeling of warmth and heaviness throughout your body, which makes you feel deeply relaxed, healthy, and peaceful.

When to Use It: Practice Self-Suggestion twice a day for about 10 minutes each time until you get good at it. You can also use it at bedtime to help yourself relax and slip easily into sleep.

Why It Can Help: Just like You're the Coach, Self-Suggestion works because your thoughts can change the way your body feels. This is another way of using your mind to make your body feel good!

What You Need: You need a quiet place, a positive attitude, and a commitment to practice.

How to Do It: Lie on your back on the floor or in bed (later, as you get better at Self-Suggestion, you can do it sitting or even standing up). Take six Belly Breaths to start to relax yourself. Then, softly repeat the first sentence below to yourself at least six times, focusing on your arms. Let any thoughts pass right through your mind—just let them go. If thoughts occur to you, gently bring your attention back to your body and your breathing. Do the same thing with the next sentence, focusing on your legs, and then with each of the next three sentences. Repeat each sentence six times slowly.

My arms feel warm and heavy.
My legs feel warm and heavy.
My stomach feels warm and heavy.
My neck and shoulders feel warm and heavy.
I am relaxed.

Even more than other B³ skills, it takes practice and time to get good at Self-Suggestion. Keep working, and you will be rewarded with a great ability to relax deeply and sleep soundly.

Have you ever walked into the kitchen after a bad day and noticed that you felt better once you smelled the comforting smells of dinner (or cookies!) in the oven? The change was real—you didn't imagine it! Good smells can actually help you feel better in many ways, including feeling more relaxed and comfortable. And that's what Aromatherapy is: using smells to help you feel better. In Aromatherapy, you use oils called "essential oils" that come from plants like lavender, peppermint, and rosemary, and also from fruits like orange, lime, and lemon.

Minty!

Sniff...sniff

When to Use It: Use Aromatherapy whenever you want to feel relaxed and comfortable, or whenever you want to fall asleep. It's helpful to smell your favorite oil at the same time you are doing a relaxation exercise such as Belly Breathing or Imagine That! They work well together to get your body even more relaxed than either one can do alone.

Why It Can Help: The nerve from your nose has a connection to deep areas of your brain. That connection has a powerful effect on how your body feels.

Sniff...sniff

Fruity!

TeA

Chamomile (KA-muh-meal) is an herb that can help with sleep. Many adults drink chamomile tea, which is safe for kids to drink, too. Just like smelling essential oils, drinking chamomile tea can have a strong relaxing effect on how your body feels.

B³

What You Need: You need high-quality essential oils, which you can buy at health food stores, at natural food co-ops, at some drug stores, and on the Internet. Ask for medical type oils so you know they are of good quality. Look for oils that say "organic" on them—that means they should be all natural.

Here's a list of what different oils can help with:

✚ For relaxation and better sleep, use sweet orange, lavender, and sandalwood.

✚ For pain, use rosemary, chamomile, and peppermint.

✚ For extra energy when you're tired, use lemon, lime, or grapefruit.

Important:
To be safe, get a parent or another adult to help you buy aromatherapy oils and do this

Essential oils

How to Do It: Unscrew the cap from the bottle, hold it about one inch from your nostrils, and inhale slowly and deeply. Repeat once or twice. Each time you inhale, imagine the healing scent traveling into your brain and sending out healing messages to your body. To enjoy oils any time, all day long, place one or two drops of oil on a tissue or cotton ball and carry it with you. Then you can smell it several times a day.

Chamomile

Sniff...sniff

If you spill essential oil, be sure to wear gloves when you wipe it up, because the oil could irritate your skin. If you get some oil on your skin, put a little vegetable oil on it and wipe it off (gently). If you accidentally splash oil in your eyes, flush your eyes with milk (whole milk if you can) and then rinse them with water. Get medical attention right away.

Skill 6: Acupressure

Acupressure was developed in East Asia (countries like China and Japan) about 5,000 years ago. It means applying pressure to specific spots on your body that can help you feel better. For example, if you feel nervous, there is a very powerful point between your eyes (see the diagram on page 45) that can relax you just by pushing on it. You have more than 300 of these spots all over your body for treating all kinds of symptoms, including problems sleeping.

Traditional Chinese culture describes a life force, or "Qi" (pronounced "chee"), that flows through each person on special pathways. When these pathways become blocked, **Acupressure** can unblock them so your Qi flows freely, making you feel more energized and healthy.

When to Use It: You can push on your acupressure points any time you want to feel more relaxed. You can also push on them throughout the day, even when you are well rested, just to keep things in balance.

Why It Can Help: Each acupressure point is connected by your nervous system to a place in your brain that controls a particular symptom (like stomachaches, sore throat, anxious feelings, or not being able to sleep). Pressing on the right acupressure point helps the body release its own feel-good chemicals (endorphins) to relieve that symptom. Stimulating these points also reduces tension and stress, relaxes muscles, and allows better blood flow. That helps oxygen and nutrients move through your body, and strengthens your immune system, too!

What You Need: You can stimulate these special acupressure points using
+ your finger
    + a pencil eraser
        + an acupressure band or beads
            + a wooden acupressure tool

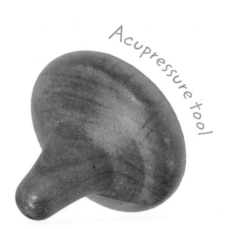

Acupressure tool

43

How to Do It: Look at the acupressure points diagrams on the next page and select a point you want to stimulate. There are several points that can help with sleep, but a good one to start with is the Third Eye Point, which is located directly between your eyebrows, in the indentation where the bridge of your nose meets your forehead. Once you've selected a point, push on it using your finger, an acupressure tool, or another tool for 30 seconds to one minute. Use medium pressure, making small circles. Repeat this every 15 minutes and take a few Belly Breaths after each stimulation. Try all the points until you find the ones that work best for you.

Acupressure can help you relax immediately, but doing it regularly can help you develop a healthier overall sleeping pattern.

Get your **Imagine That!** skill involved, too. As you press on one of your points, imagine your finger or acupressure tool is sending healing energy into that spot.

Third Eye Point

Between your eyebrows, in the dip where the top of your nose and the bottom of your forehead meet, this point relaxes your nerves and helps you sleep.

Inner Gate

Located in the middle of the inside of your wrist, two and one-half finger widths above your wrist crease, this point relaxes your nerves and helps you sleep.

Sea of Energy

This point, located three finger widths below your belly button, can refresh you when your body feels weak or overly tired.

Spirit Gate

This point, found on the inside of your wrist crease, in line with your little finger, can help settle you down if you're very excited.

Joyful Sleep

This point, located just below the inside of your anklebone, can help you get to sleep.

Three Mile Point

Found just on the outside of your shinbone four finger widths below your knee cap, this point can refresh you when your body feels weak or overly tired.

45

Skill 7: Massage

For thousands of years, human touch has been used all over the world to heal people and make them feel better. Massage means pushing, pulling, and putting pressure on muscles and skin. This helps calm the nerves, relax tight muscles, improve blood flow, and reduce pain. Massage can be very relaxing and help you sleep.

When to Use It: Use Massage whenever you want to feel relaxed and comfortable, or whenever you want to fall asleep.

Why It Can Help: Massage relaxes your muscles, makes you more comfortable, and calms your nerves.

What You Need: You can use a small amount of lotion or oil (like baby oil), but you don't need to.

How to Do It: Here are three short Massages that can help you relax and sleep better. You can do each one by yourself or have another person do them to you.

Toes. Start by gently rubbing and pushing on the backs of your ankles. Then move to your heels, again gently rubbing and pushing, and then do the same to the ball of your foot. Finally, gently squeeze each toe separately.

Stomach area. Using gentle pressure, move the tips of your fingers in a circle about two or three inches around your belly button.

Your head. Gently press with your fingers or thumbs on the back of your head at the base of your skull. Then move up the center of your head, applying gentle pressure to your scalp over the back and then the top of your head. Gently rub the temples and forehead.

Keep Practicing

Once you have practiced all the B³ skills a few times, figure out which ones work best for you. Maybe you like using them all. If so, great! Whichever skills you use, remember to keep practicing them regularly, even when you are feeling fine, so you're comfortable with them and they become part of your everyday life. That way you'll be able to use them easily when you have trouble sleeping. You'll also prevent some sleep problems from starting in the first place.

Feel Good Every Day

Earlier in this book you learned how sleep (and sleep problems) can affect your waking life in many ways. It's also true that things you feel and do during the day have a huge effect on your sleep. One way to improve your sleep is to improve your lifestyle habits. "Lifestyle" means all the basic things you do every day, like exercising, eating, doing activities, going to school, and enjoying hobbies. Because you do these things every day, they're a big part of your life. If you make changes in your lifestyle you can do a lot to feel healthier and more relaxed and sleep better. Check out these ideas for getting healthier in several lifestyle areas. To begin with, choose two or three areas where you would like to improve, and try some of the ideas. Later, you can improve other areas. Even small changes can make a big difference!

Move More, Feel Better: Exercise

● Do something active by yourself—like walking, biking, or swimming—for at least 15 minutes, five days a week.

● Play team sports such as soccer, lacrosse, volleyball, or basketball. ● Get flexible. Try yoga, dance, gymnastics, or tai chi.

● Include activity in plans you make with friends or family: go to the zoo, go sightseeing, play with pets, rake leaves, take walks.

Eat Well and Feel Super: Your Diet

- Eat a broad variety of foods including lots of fruits and vegetables of different colors. A variety of foods means a variety of nutrients for your body.
- Eating smaller meals and snacks regularly throughout the day may be better than eating large amounts of food less often, because it helps your energy level stay even. ● Drink plenty of water every day to keep your body working its best.
- Eat more **whole foods** and fewer **processed foods** (whole foods are fresh, natural foods that haven't been changed or prepared; foods that *have* been changed or prepared are processed). Whole foods provide more nutrients and none of the unhelpful extra stuff that comes in processed foods (like artificial dyes and sweeteners).
- Eat organic foods (natural foods that have been grown without the use of artificial chemicals) whenever possible.

Give Yourself a Break: Life Management

- Don't commit yourself to too many activities. Even if all the things you're doing are fun, you can really wear yourself out if you don't have enough downtime.
- You don't have to be perfect or be the best at everything you do. It's important to do as well as you can at things, but try to remember that nobody is perfect. ● Limit your screen time (TV, computers, video games) to no more than one hour a day on weekdays and two hours a day on weekends. Too much screen time keeps you from getting exercise and connecting with others. And, too much screen time close to bedtime can get you too wound up to sleep.

49

Take Care of Your Inner Self: Spiritual Stuff

- Take pause. Spend 15 minutes each day on quiet reflection, prayer, or meditation. • Keep a "Gratitude Journal." Every day, write down three things you are thankful for. Also, tell someone in your life why you appreciate him or her.
- Enjoy nature. Take a stroll in a park or, if you can, walk through woods, or by a lake or river. Enjoy gardens and flowers along city streets. • Find and appreciate beauty. Go to art galleries or museums or listen to music. • Create. Paint, draw, sculpt with clay, play music, or do crafts. • Volunteer to help. Helping and supporting others feels great.

Sleeping is part of your lifestyle, too. You can use B^3 skills to help with your sleep, but you can also develop regular, daily lifestyle habits to improve your sleep. An important first step is going to bed at the same time every night, even on weekends. Have a bedtime routine that doesn't change. For example, brush your teeth, wash your face, and listen to relaxing music. Don't watch TV, get on a computer, or instant message—these are stimulating and can keep you from winding down. Sleep in a cool, quiet, dark room without any computer screens, televisions, or lamps on (a night light is okay). In the morning, make sure to get exposed to natural light as soon as possible to help set your body clock to your wake and sleep schedule.

Connect with People: Social Supports

- Have a good laugh with family and friends every day—tell jokes, watch a silly movie or TV show, check out a funny Web site, or put on a goofy play together.
- Do activities with family or friends. For example, play games, play sports, or go to the movies. • Eat breakfast, lunch, or dinner with friends and/or family. Don't have the TV on or anything else that could distract you during the meal. Don't answer the phone, either. Instead, pay attention to each other. Take your time, relax, and talk. • Hang out with friends outside of school. Play and have fun. If you're too busy, call them up to say hello.

Keep Track of Your Progress

Being the boss of your body gives you a lot of power over your health, but you have to stick with it. It can be a slow process at first, but if you don't give up and you continue to practice, you'll get better at the B³ skills—and you'll feel better and better.

To help yourself stay excited and confident about being the boss of your body, even when it seems hard, keep track of your progress. This helps show you that you *are* getting better, even if sometimes it doesn't feel like it. Remember your whole-self checkup on pages 18–25? Do those exercises every day and notice how your feelings change. Stick stickers (or write "B³") on your family calendar or your notebook pages when you do B³ activities. That helps you see how much you're doing and reminds you to keep at it. It won't be long before you'll see some real improvement.

Stick with It!

You have a lot to be proud of: you have tons of natural talent to balance and heal yourself and live healthier. With a positive attitude and a commitment to practice, you have everything you need to

- be the boss of your sleep
- be the boss of your body
- **and be the boss of your life!**

A Note to Grown-Ups

When children suffer from sleep problems, their nights *and* days can be downright miserable. It's hard to have fun or do activities. Home, school, and other responsibilities may be done poorly or ignored completely. The worst part, for many of us, is feeling like there's nothing we can do to ease a child's suffering. But we *can* help kids cope with sleep problems.

The self-care skills in this book are a powerful tool children can use on their own to take control of their health and wellness—including their sleep. Studies show that kids who have practiced these skills and who feel confident about their role in their health and wellness handle sleep problems (and other health issues) more easily than kids who don't. By encouraging the children you know to read this book and practice the skills in it, you are giving them a great gift that they can use the rest of their lives.

About Self-Care Skills

As recently as 30 years ago, it was not widely accepted (in Western medicine) that people could control physical activities like their breathing, heart rate, blood pressure, skin temperature, or perspiration rate. Now, we not only know that people can control these (all of which influence our experiences of relaxation and our ability to sleep well) but also that the way people think about their health or illness has a lot to do with how they feel physically. We also know that skills like the ones in this book can have a huge ongoing impact on people's health.

Surgery, medicine, and other medical interventions all have their place and are sometimes necessary. However, much of the time self-care skills are a safer, less invasive, more natural—and self-directed—way for people to lead healthy lives. Kids and families can create and maintain an optimal level of health and wellness by using these skills and by making improvements to lifestyle aspects such as diet, sleep, and exercise.

Your Role as a Coach

The Be the Boss of Your Body (B³) series is about kids taking charge of their own health, but that doesn't mean kids don't need help from adults. Adults who help kids with the B³ skills are called coaches. Any caring adult can be a coach to a child struggling with sleep—including a parent, grandparent, sibling, healthcare professional, school nurse, teacher, or friend. Being a coach means supporting the child in the process of learning these skills and making lifestyle changes. Kids need encouragement when the process seems hard or slow; they need positive reinforcement when they practice; and they need love and support when they are not feeling well.

What are the most important things you can do to provide this support?

- Read this book to gain a better understanding of what your child is doing.
- Be available and supportive when your child feels uncomfortable.
- Believe what your child tells you about how he or she feels.
- Give your child as much control as possible to manage his or her sleep.
- Give praise and positive reinforcement for using the skills; celebrate successes.
- Encourage your child to continue participating in school and favorite activities.
- Engage in self-care skills yourself.
- Recognize that everyone is different—your child's way of managing sleep may be different from yours.

Evidence suggests that people who engage in self-care activities live healthier, more productive lives. Teaching kids to look at their health from a holistic perspective— considering body, mind, and spirit—and teaching them self-care skills sets the stage for lifelong wellness and balance. By encouraging and helping your children with the skills in this book, and modeling the skills yourself, you can give them the confidence to uncover the wealth of talent and strength they possess and encourage them to actively participate in their health. These skills can make a positive difference in *your* life, too!

Please remember that this book is not intended as a replacement for professional medical or psychological consultation when this is needed. Children and adolescents who are having serious health problems or new onset symptoms should be evaluated by their primary care provider. Problems that are acute, severe, and/or associated with other symptoms such as pain, fever, nausea, or rash need to be evaluated and treated by a qualified healthcare professional.

Glossary

acupressure: applying pressure to specific spots on your body to help you feel better. Go to pages 42–45 to learn how to do it.

aromatherapy: using healing smells from natural plant oils to help you feel better. Go to pages 38–41 to learn more.

balance: you are balanced when your mind, body, and spirit are healthy and positive, adding up to a whole, healthy, fabulous you! Check out pages 8–9 to learn more about what this feels like.

endorphins: natural chemicals your body releases to reduce pain. You can learn ways to get your body to release endorphins on pages 28 and 43.

essential oils: oils that give plants their smells and that are used in aromatherapy. To read more, go to pages 38–41.

self-care: things you can do yourself to take care of yourself. That's what this book is about!

spirit: the part of you, deep inside, that gives you feelings of hope, comfort, and peace and gives life meaning. Go to page 7 to learn more.

About the Authors

Timothy Culbert, M.D., is a behavioral and developmental pediatrician with training in biofeedback, medical hypnosis, and holistic medicine. He is the medical director for the Integrative Medicine Program at Children's Hospitals and Clinics of Minnesota. Tim gives presentations nationally and internationally and publishes widely on mind-body skills training with children and teens. He has helped kids in clinical practice for 15 years, with special interests in teaching kids self-care skills.

Tim lives in Greenwood, Minnesota, with his wife, Heidi, and teenage children, Sam and Hannah. He enjoys traveling, cooking, writing, hiking, and various creative endeavors.

Rebecca Kajander, C.P.N.P., M.P.H., is a nurse practitioner at the Alexander Center, Park Nicollet Health Services of Minnesota. She has treated children and adolescents for nearly 40 years, has helped hundreds of children take care of themselves using self-care skills, and helped many more understand and live with ADHD. In 2000, Rebecca was named "Pediatric Nurse Practitioner of the Year" by the Minnesota chapter of the National Association of Pediatric Nurse Practitioners.

Rebecca has been a lifelong resident of Minnetonka, Minnesota. She's married and has a grown son. When not working, Rebecca enjoys yoga and doing just about anything outdoors.